Using a HELOC to Build Wealth

How Smart Homeowners Fund Businesses, Investments, and Passive Income

By Joseph G. Correa

Licensed Mortgage Broker, Finibi Mortgage

Copyright & Legal Notice

First Edition, 2026

Table of Contents

Foreword 5

Chapter 1: Turning Home Equity Into an Investment Engine 10

Chapter 2: Designing a Wealth-Building HELOC Strategy 16

Chapter 3: Scaling Wealth With HELOC Recycling 21

Chapter 4: Selecting the Right Investments for HELOC Capital 26

Chapter 5: Protecting Your Home While Using It to Build Wealth 30

Chapter 6: Using HELOCs to Build Passive Income for Life 34

Chapter 7: Accelerating Wealth Through Strategic Reinvestment 38

Chapter 8: Building a Long-Term Wealth Flywheel With a HELOC 41

Chapter 9: Knowing When to Pause, Pay Down, and Lock in Gains 45

Chapter 10: Turning Home Equity Into a Legacy of Wealth 49

Chapter 11: Exiting the HELOC While Keeping the Wealth 52

Chapter 12: Living on HELOC-Built Wealth Without Going Back to Work55

Chapter 13: Rebuilding, Repeating, and Expanding the Wealth Cycle 58

Chapter 14: Creating Financial Freedom With a HELOC Lifestyle 62

Chapter 15: Making Your HELOC Wealth System Bulletproof 65

Final Thoughts 68

How to Get a Personalized HELOC Review..71

Foreword

The purpose of this book is to change how you see your home forever. Most people think of their house as a place to live, a roof over their head, or at best a long-term retirement asset they might someday sell. But in reality, for homeowners who understand how money actually works, a home is one of the most powerful wealth-building engines ever created. It is one of the only assets that can legally be leveraged at extremely low interest rates, with tax-advantaged treatment, flexible repayment, and no required liquidation schedule. In other words, your home is not just a place to live — it is a private bank, a funding source, and a financial accelerator. This book exists to show you how sophisticated investors, entrepreneurs, and financially free families use home equity not to survive, but to multiply their income, build businesses, acquire cash-flowing assets, and create long-term wealth that compounds for decades.

Most homeowners never learn this because the financial system is not designed to teach it. Banks, brokers, and even financial advisors often focus on selling products, not building wealth. You are taught to save, to avoid debt, and to slowly invest in paper assets while your largest financial asset — your home — sits idle. Meanwhile, the wealthy quietly use leverage to buy income, control assets, and move faster than savers ever could. A HELOC, when used properly, allows you to convert trapped equity into working capital. It gives you access to money that can buy businesses, fund investments, create passive income streams, or generate returns far greater than the interest you pay. This is not reckless borrowing. This is disciplined, strategic capital deployment, and it is how real wealth is built.

This book does not promote speculation or gambling. It is not about chasing hot stocks, crypto hype, or risky ventures. It is about using home equity the way banks use money: to deploy capital into income-producing assets that pay themselves back and then continue generating cash long after the original funds are repaid. Whether you want to start a small business, buy rental properties, invest in private lending, purchase cash-flowing digital assets, or build a portfolio of passive income streams, a HELOC can become your lowest-cost, most flexible source of capital. When structured correctly, your home becomes the engine that funds your entire financial future.

One of the most misunderstood ideas in personal finance is the difference between consumer debt and productive debt. Credit cards, car loans, and personal loans are usually used to buy depreciating items that drain cash from your life. A HELOC, when used to build wealth, is different. It is a tool to acquire assets that create cash flow. The moment you use borrowed money to buy something that pays you back more than it costs, debt stops being dangerous and starts becoming powerful. The wealthy do not fear leverage — they fear unproductive leverage. This book teaches you how to use leverage with precision, discipline, and a clear return-on-investment mindset.

As a licensed mortgage broker working with homeowners, investors, and entrepreneurs across the country, I have watched countless people transform their lives by learning this one principle: money that sits still loses, money that moves and produces wins. Home equity sitting in a property does nothing for you. It does not pay bills. It does not grow. It does not create freedom. But when deployed into the right investments, that same equity can produce income that covers mortgages, pays for college, funds retirements, and creates generational wealth. I have seen families replace full-time incomes, business owners scale faster than their competitors, and investors build portfolios that would have taken decades through savings alone.

This book is your bridge from understanding HELOCs to mastering them as a wealth-building tool. You already learned how HELOCs work, how to qualify, how to manage credit, and how to control risk in the earlier books of this series. Now you are ready for the most important stage: putting that power to work. This is where strategy replaces fear. This is where planning replaces guesswork. This is where your home stops being a passive asset and starts becoming an active wealth engine.

You will learn how to think like a capital allocator, not just a borrower. You will learn how to evaluate investments, compare returns, structure deals, and design cash-flow systems that safely recycle your HELOC over and over again. You will learn how to build multiple income streams instead of relying on a single paycheck. You will learn how to turn your home into the foundation of a financial ecosystem that supports your lifestyle, your family, and your long-term goals. This is not theory — it is how many of the most financially free people in the world operate, even if they never talk about it publicly.

The goal is not to take on more debt. The goal is to own more income. When done correctly, the investments funded by your HELOC pay down the line itself, while continuing to produce profits. Over time, your risk drops, your equity grows, and your cash flow expands. This is how people escape the paycheck-to-paycheck cycle. This is how they stop worrying about inflation, interest rates, or job security. They build systems that generate money no matter what the economy does.

Book 8 exists because this is the missing piece in most people's financial lives. They may have equity, they may have good credit, and they may even have a HELOC — but they do not have a plan. A HELOC without a strategy is just another line of credit. A HELOC with a wealth-building blueprint becomes a financial superpower. My mission is to give you that blueprint, so you can use your home the way it was always meant to be used — not just as shelter, but as the cornerstone of your financial independence.

As you move through this book, approach it with an open mind and a long-term vision. You are not just reading about borrowing. You are learning how to create opportunity, scale income, and design a life that is not controlled by a single paycheck, a single employer, or a single economic cycle. This is how smart homeowners think. This is how they build lasting wealth. And this is how you will learn to do the same.

Chapter 1

Turning Home Equity Into an Investment Engine

Most homeowners believe wealth is created by saving money, but in reality wealth is created by deploying capital into assets that produce more money. The problem is that most people never have enough free capital to do this at scale. Their cash is tied up in bills, mortgages, and living expenses. Yet for millions of homeowners, the largest pool of capital they already own sits locked inside their house. Home equity is not just a number on a statement. It is dormant financial energy. When accessed through a properly structured HELOC, that energy can be transformed into working capital that builds businesses, buys assets, and generates cash flow. This chapter teaches you how to view your HELOC not as a loan, but as an investment engine.

A HELOC gives you revolving access to capital that can be borrowed, repaid, and borrowed again. That makes it fundamentally different from a traditional loan. When used to invest, this revolving feature allows you to recycle the same money over and over, compounding your results. If you borrow $100,000 from a HELOC and invest it into an asset that produces income, and that income pays the HELOC back, you still own the asset. Once the HELOC is paid down, you can draw that same $100,000 again to invest in something else. Over time, one pool of equity can fund multiple assets that all generate income. This is how leverage, when used properly, multiplies wealth.

The key principle behind using a HELOC to build wealth is spread. Spread is the difference between what your money earns and what your money costs. If your HELOC costs you 8 percent per year but your investments produce 15 percent per year, you have a positive spread of 7 percent. That spread is pure wealth creation. You are using borrowed money to create income that exceeds the cost of borrowing. This is exactly how banks operate. They borrow money at a low rate from depositors and lend it out at a higher rate to borrowers. Your HELOC allows you to do the same thing using your home as the capital base.

However, this only works when you invest in cash-flowing assets, not speculative ones. Cash flow is the money that shows up in your account every month regardless of what the market does. Rental properties, private lending, small businesses, dividend-paying investments, and digital assets that generate revenue are examples of cash-flowing investments. Appreciation is a bonus, but cash flow is what pays the HELOC, reduces risk, and keeps the system running. When you use a HELOC to buy cash flow, the asset does the work of paying back the debt.

The most powerful part of this strategy is velocity. When your investments produce monthly income, that income can be applied directly to your HELOC balance. This reduces your interest costs and frees up available credit faster. The faster your HELOC gets paid down, the faster you can redeploy the capital into the next investment. Over time, this creates a flywheel effect where your money moves faster and faster, producing more income each cycle. This is how one home can quietly fund an entire portfolio of income streams.

Risk management is what separates smart HELOC investors from reckless ones. You never want to use your HELOC to fund anything that does not produce income or that you cannot reasonably control. You also want to keep a cash buffer so that even if an investment underperforms, you can still service the HELOC. When structured correctly, the risk of losing your home is extremely low because the investments themselves are paying the debt. The danger comes from using HELOCs for consumption instead of production.

This chapter gives you the framework. Your HELOC is not just borrowed money. It is capital. Capital is a tool. When that tool is used to acquire income-producing assets with positive spread and disciplined cash flow, it becomes a wealth-building machine that can operate for decades. You are no longer dependent on savings or slow pay raises. You are operating a financial system.

Practical Example: *How a HELOC Creates Real Wealth With Numbers*

Imagine a homeowner named Maria who owns a home worth $500,000 and has a mortgage balance of $300,000. This means she has $200,000 in equity. A lender offers her a HELOC at 80 percent loan-to-value. Eighty percent of $500,000 is $400,000. When we subtract her existing $300,000 mortgage, she qualifies for a $100,000 HELOC. This gives Maria access to $100,000 in revolving capital while still living in her home.

Maria decides to use $80,000 of her HELOC to invest. The HELOC interest rate is 8 percent annually, which means the yearly cost on $80,000 is $6,400. Divided by twelve months, that is about $533 per month in interest. Now Maria invests the $80,000 into a combination of a small rental property down payment and a private lending deal that together produce $1,200 per month in net cash flow after all expenses.

Every month, Maria receives $1,200 in income. She uses $533 of that to cover the HELOC interest. That leaves $667 per month as profit. Instead of spending that profit, she applies it directly to the HELOC principal. After twelve months, she has paid $8,004 toward the HELOC balance, because $667 times twelve equals $8,004. This reduces her HELOC from $80,000 down to $71,996.

At the same time, Maria still owns the rental property and the private lending note. They continue producing $1,200 per month. In the second year, she repeats the process. The interest is now slightly lower because the balance is lower, and she continues paying down principal. Over five years, the investment income completely pays off the $80,000 HELOC draw. Yet Maria still owns the investments that are now producing $1,200 per month for her.

This means Maria used borrowed money to buy assets that paid for themselves. She did not use her own savings. Her home's equity funded the deal, and the investments eliminated the debt. After five years, Maria now has an extra $1,200 per month, or $14,400 per year, in passive income. That income is now hers forever as long as she owns the assets.

Now comes the compounding effect. Because her HELOC is paid back, she can draw on it again. She could use another $80,000 to buy more cash-flowing assets and repeat the cycle. After another five years, she could have $2,400 per month in income. After another cycle, $3,600 per month. One house, one HELOC, and disciplined investing can quietly create a six-figure income stream over time.

This is why using a HELOC to build wealth is not about debt. It is about controlled leverage. Maria's home did not become riskier over time. It became safer because the investments created income that could pay any obligation. Her net worth increased, her cash flow increased, and her financial stress decreased.

This is the power of turning home equity into an investment engine. When you use borrowed money to buy income instead of expenses, the math works in your favor. The numbers are not magic. They are simply the result of positive spread, disciplined cash flow, and a system that lets your home quietly fund your future.

Chapter 2

Designing a Wealth-Building HELOC Strategy

Using a HELOC to build wealth is not about randomly investing money. It is about designing a system that safely turns equity into income. A system has rules, structure, and feedback loops that keep it stable even when markets change. Without a strategy, a HELOC becomes just another loan. With a strategy, it becomes a financial machine that funds growth while protecting the homeowner. This chapter teaches you how to design that system so your home becomes a long-term wealth engine instead of a financial liability.

The first rule of a wealth-building HELOC is that every dollar borrowed must have a job. You do not draw funds simply because they are available. You draw them because there is a specific income-producing opportunity waiting. This mindset is what separates investors from consumers. Consumers borrow first and hope they figure it out later. Investors line up the deal first and then pull the money only when it is ready to be deployed. This keeps risk low and ensures that your HELOC is always tied to an asset, not a lifestyle expense. The second rule is diversification of income, not debt. A single investment may work well, but a portfolio of income streams is what creates stability. When you use a HELOC, you should aim to spread your capital across different types of assets that do not all depend on the same market. A rental property, a private lending note, and a small digital business do not all rise and fall together. If one underperforms, the others continue producing income. This reduces the chance that a single problem can disrupt your ability to pay the HELOC.

The third rule is cash-flow coverage. Your investments should produce significantly more cash flow than the minimum HELOC payment. This creates a margin of safety. If your HELOC costs $500 per month, you should aim for investments that produce $800 to $1,000 per month. That extra cash gives you breathing room and allows you to pay down the HELOC faster. The faster you reduce the balance, the faster you regain borrowing power and lower risk.

The fourth rule is velocity of money. When cash flow comes in, it should not sit idle. It should be used to reduce your HELOC balance or be reinvested. Idle money is lost opportunity. When income pays down the HELOC, it creates new available credit. That new available credit can be redeployed into more income-producing assets. This recycling effect is how one HELOC can fund many investments over time. The fifth rule is control. You should prioritize investments where you can influence the outcome. Rental properties can be improved.

Private lending can be structured with collateral. Small businesses can be optimized. You are not at the mercy of a stock price or a market crash. Control is what allows you to protect your home while still using leverage.

When these rules are combined, a HELOC stops being a risk and becomes a tool. You are no longer gambling with your house. You are operating a business that uses equity as working capital. The strategy is what keeps everything balanced. Without it, leverage becomes dangerous. With it, leverage becomes powerful.

Practical Example: *Building a HELOC Wealth System With Real Numbers*

Let's look at David, a homeowner with a $600,000 home and a $350,000 mortgage. That gives him $250,000 in equity. At 80 percent loan-to-value, his maximum loan is $480,000. Subtracting his $350,000 mortgage, David qualifies for a $130,000 HELOC. He decides to use $100,000 of it to start building income.

His HELOC interest rate is 8 percent. Eight percent of $100,000 is $8,000 per year, which is about $667 per month. David does not invest all $100,000 into one deal. Instead, he follows the diversification rule. He puts $50,000 into a small rental property down payment that produces $600 per month in net cash flow. He puts $30,000 into a private lending deal that pays him $400 per month in interest. He uses the remaining $20,000 to buy a small online business that generates $300 per month in profit.

David's total monthly income from these three investments is $1,300. His HELOC cost is $667. When he subtracts $667 from $1,300, he is left with $633 per month. That $633 is applied directly to the HELOC balance. After one year, he pays $7,596 toward the HELOC principal because $633 times twelve equals $7,596. His HELOC balance drops from $100,000 to $92,404.

In year two, the interest cost drops slightly because the balance is lower. His income stays at $1,300. His cash flow continues paying down the HELOC. Over five years, David pays off nearly all of the $100,000. Yet his rental property, private lending note, and online business still exist and still generate $1,300 per month.

This means David has turned home equity into permanent income. He did not save $100,000. He used his home's equity to create $15,600 per year in cash flow. Once the HELOC is paid off, that income becomes his. He can then repeat the process and build another layer of income using the same HELOC.

This is how the math works when strategy is applied. Each investment adds income. That income reduces debt. Reduced debt creates more available credit. That credit funds more income. Over time, the system compounds. David's home becomes the foundation of a financial engine that can grow for the rest of his life.

Chapter 3

Scaling Wealth With HELOC Recycling

Once you understand how to turn home equity into income, the next step is learning how to scale it. Scaling means using the same money multiple times to build more assets without increasing your long-term risk. This is where most homeowners either unlock extraordinary results or make costly mistakes. A HELOC gives you revolving capital, but only when you pair that revolving feature with cash-flowing investments does it become a compounding machine. The goal is not to stay in debt. The goal is to let debt temporarily fund assets that permanently produce income.

Recycling a HELOC means borrowing, investing, paying the balance down, and then borrowing again to fund another income-producing asset. Each cycle adds another layer of cash flow to your financial life. The mistake people make is leaving the HELOC permanently maxed out. When the line is always full, risk is high and flexibility is low. When the line is constantly being paid down by investment income, your available credit grows while your risk shrinks. This is the heart of HELOC-based wealth building. The speed at which you recycle matters. The faster your investments pay down your HELOC, the faster you regain borrowing power. This is why cash flow is more important than appreciation. An asset that rises in value but produces no income does nothing to help you recycle capital. An asset that produces steady monthly income accelerates the entire system. When income reduces the HELOC balance, interest costs fall, available credit increases, and the system becomes safer and more powerful at the same time.

Another key concept is stacking. Stacking means that each new investment is layered on top of the last one. You do not replace income, you add to it. The first investment might produce $500 per month. The second adds another $500. The third adds another $500. Over time, these layers of income create financial stability. Even if one investment struggles, the others continue producing. Your HELOC is no longer supported by a single asset but by a portfolio.

Recycling also requires discipline. When you receive cash flow, you must choose to send it back to the HELOC instead of spending it. This is where most people fail. They treat the income as lifestyle money instead of system money. When you delay consumption and focus on reducing the HELOC, you are effectively buying future freedom. Every dollar that reduces your HELOC today creates more investing power tomorrow.

Over time, something remarkable happens. Your HELOC balance trends downward while your income trends upward. The risk of leverage declines even as your wealth grows. Eventually, you reach a point where your cash-flowing assets are so strong that even if the HELOC were fully drawn, the income could easily service it. At that point, your home is no longer a risk. It is the foundation of a financial empire.

This is the long-term vision of HELOC recycling. It is not about one deal. It is about building a system that turns equity into income, income into credit, and credit into even more income. When done correctly, it creates a compounding effect that few people ever experience.

Practical Example: *Recycling a HELOC Into a Growing Income Stream*

Let's look at Angela, who owns a home worth $550,000 and has a $300,000 mortgage. That gives her $250,000 in equity. At 80 percent loan-to-value, her maximum loan is $440,000. Subtracting her mortgage, she qualifies for a $140,000 HELOC. She starts by using $70,000 to invest in income-producing assets.

Her HELOC rate is 8 percent. Eight percent of $70,000 is $5,600 per year, or about $467 per month. Angela invests the $70,000 into two assets. She uses $40,000 as a down payment on a small rental that produces $600 per month in net cash flow. She uses $30,000 to fund a private lending deal that pays her $350 per month in interest. Her total monthly income from these two investments is $950.

Angela takes the $950 and pays the $467 HELOC interest first. That leaves $483 per month. She applies that $483 directly to the HELOC balance. After one year, she has paid $5,796 toward the HELOC principal because $483 times twelve equals $5,796. Her HELOC balance drops from $70,000 to $64,204.

In year two, her investments still produce $950 per month. Her interest cost is slightly lower because the balance is lower. She continues applying the excess to principal. After three years, she has paid down over $17,000 of the original $70,000. Now she has new available credit. Instead of waiting, she draws another $20,000 from the HELOC and invests it into a small cash-flowing digital business that produces $250 per month.

Now Angela's income increases from $950 to $1,200 per month. Her HELOC balance rises slightly because of the new draw, but her income has grown. She continues sending the surplus to the HELOC. Over time, all three investments work together to pay down the balance.

After several years, Angela owns three income-producing assets funded by the same original equity. Her HELOC may fluctuate, but her income keeps increasing. Eventually, the line is paid down while her assets keep producing. That is the power of recycling.

Angela did not need a high salary or huge savings. She used the equity in her home, disciplined cash flow, and a recycling strategy to build lasting wealth. This is how a single HELOC becomes a long-term income engine.

Chapter 4

Selecting the Right Investments for HELOC Capital

The success or failure of using a HELOC to build wealth depends less on the HELOC itself and more on what you invest in. A HELOC is simply a tool. The real driver of results is the quality of the assets you buy with it. When the wrong investments are chosen, leverage becomes dangerous. When the right investments are chosen, leverage becomes a force multiplier that accelerates wealth. This chapter explains how to evaluate, select, and structure investments so that your home equity is always working for you instead of against you.

The first principle of HELOC investing is that income comes before growth. Appreciation is unpredictable. Cash flow is measurable. You should never use home equity to fund something that does not produce regular income. If an investment does not put money back into your account every month or every quarter, it cannot help you service the HELOC. Without cash flow, you are forced to rely on outside income to carry the debt, which increases risk. When investments pay you, they protect you. The second principle is durability. A good HELOC-funded investment should survive economic cycles. Rental housing, private lending, essential services, and basic digital infrastructure tend to perform well even when the economy slows. Luxury, trends, and speculative assets tend to collapse when conditions tighten. When your home is the collateral behind your investment capital, you must choose assets that people will still need even in hard times.

The third principle is control. You want investments where you can influence the outcome. With a rental, you can raise rents, improve the property, or change management. With a small business, you can optimize marketing and pricing. With private lending, you control the loan terms. This control gives you the ability to fix problems instead of being stuck watching them happen.

The fourth principle is exit strategy. Every investment should have a clear way out. You should always know how you would convert that asset back into cash if needed. This could mean selling a property, refinancing a loan, selling a business, or liquidating a note. Liquidity is part of risk management. You are not trapped if something changes.

The fifth principle is scalability. The best HELOC investments are those you can repeat. If one rental works, you can buy another. If one lending deal works, you can do ten more. If one digital business works, you can clone it. Scalability allows you to turn a single HELOC into a growing portfolio instead of a one-time win.

When you apply these principles together, you create a filter that eliminates most bad investments automatically. You stop asking whether something is exciting and start asking whether it produces income, survives downturns, gives you control, has an exit, and can be repeated. This is how professionals allocate capital, and this is how you protect your home while building wealth.

Practical Example: *Choosing the Right HELOC Investment Mix*

Let's look at Carla, who has a $480,000 home with a $280,000 mortgage. She has $200,000 in equity. At 80 percent loan-to-value, her maximum loan is $384,000. Subtracting her mortgage, she qualifies for a $104,000 HELOC. She decides to invest $90,000 of it while keeping $14,000 as a safety buffer.

Her HELOC rate is 8 percent, which means the yearly cost on $90,000 is $7,200. Divided by twelve months, that is $600 per month. Carla now chooses three investments based on the principles above. She puts $50,000 into a rental property down payment that produces $700 per month in net cash flow. She invests $25,000 into a private lending deal that pays her 10 percent annually, which equals $2,500 per year or about

$208 per month. She invests the remaining $15,000 into a small online business that produces $200 per month.

Carla's total monthly income from these three investments is $700 plus $208 plus $200, which equals $1,108. Her HELOC costs her $600 per month. When she subtracts $600 from $1,108, she has $508 left. She sends that $508 directly to the HELOC principal.

After one year, Carla has paid $6,096 toward the HELOC balance because $508 times twelve equals $6,096. Her HELOC balance drops from $90,000 to $83,904. Her investments are still producing the same $1,108 per month.

Over five years, Carla pays off most of the $90,000 while still owning all three income-producing assets. Once the HELOC is paid off, the $1,108 per month becomes her permanent passive income. That is $13,296 per year, created entirely from equity she already owned.

Carla did not gamble. She selected durable, cash-flowing, controllable, and scalable investments. Her home funded them. The investments paid the HELOC. The result is long-term wealth built safely and logically.

Chapter 5

Protecting Your Home While Using It to Build Wealth

Using a HELOC to build wealth can be incredibly powerful, but it must always be done with one priority above all else: protecting the home. Your home is not just collateral, it is the foundation of your financial life. The purpose of a wealth-building HELOC strategy is to turn equity into income without ever putting that foundation at risk. This chapter explains how to structure leverage, cash flow, and reserves so that even if something goes wrong, your home remains safe.

The first protection rule is never to use your HELOC for consumption. Consumption includes vacations, cars, luxury items, or lifestyle upgrades. These do not create income and therefore do not help service the debt. When people get into trouble with HELOCs, it is almost always because they borrowed against their home to buy things that disappear while the debt remains. Wealth is built when every dollar borrowed produces more money than it costs.

The second rule is cash-flow coverage. Your HELOC payments should never depend on your job. They should be paid by your investments. If your HELOC costs $600 per month, your investments should produce at least $900 to $1,200 per month. That margin is your safety net. If one investment underperforms, you still have enough income to cover the line. Excess cash flow is not greed; it is protection.

The third rule is liquidity. You must always keep part of your HELOC unused or keep cash in reserve. This gives you flexibility if something unexpected happens. If a tenant moves out, a business slows, or a payment is late, you still have access to funds to make the HELOC payment without stress. Liquidity is what prevents panic.

The fourth rule is diversification. No single investment should support the entire HELOC. If you have three or four income streams paying into the line, one problem cannot collapse the system. Diversification spreads risk and stabilizes your financial structure.

The fifth rule is principal reduction. Your investments should not only pay the interest; they should also reduce the HELOC balance over time. This continuously lowers your risk and increases your available credit. The more the balance goes down, the safer the strategy becomes.

When all five rules are followed, your home is not in danger. In fact, it becomes safer because it is supported by multiple streams of income instead of a single paycheck. This is the difference between reckless borrowing and strategic leverage.

Practical Example: *How Safety Is Built Into a HELOC Wealth Plan*

Let's look at Robert, who owns a home worth $520,000 and has a $300,000 mortgage. He has $220,000 in equity. At 80 percent loan-to-value, his maximum loan is $416,000. Subtracting his mortgage, he qualifies for a $116,000 HELOC. He decides to only use $80,000 of it, keeping $36,000 as a safety buffer.

His HELOC interest rate is 8 percent. Eight percent of $80,000 is $6,400 per year, or about $533 per month. Robert invests the $80,000 into three income streams. He uses $45,000 as a rental property down payment that produces $650 per month. He uses $20,000 in private lending that pays him $250 per month. He uses $15,000 in a small online business that produces $200 per month. His total monthly income is $1,100.

Robert uses $533 of that to pay the HELOC interest. That leaves $567 per month. He applies that $567 to the HELOC principal. Over one year, that equals $6,804 because $567 times twelve is $6,804. His HELOC balance drops from $80,000 to $73,196.

At the same time, he still has $36,000 in unused HELOC credit as a reserve. Even if one investment stops producing for a few months, he can use that buffer to make payments. His home is protected because the system does not depend on perfect performance.

After five years, Robert's investments have paid off most of the $80,000 while still producing $1,100 per month. His HELOC is nearly zero, but his income continues. That is safety through structure, not luck.

Chapter 6

Using HELOCs to Build Passive Income for Life

The ultimate goal of using a HELOC to build wealth is not just to grow your net worth, but to create passive income that supports you for the rest of your life. Passive income is money that continues to arrive whether you are working or not. It is what turns financial survival into financial freedom. A HELOC, when used correctly, is one of the most powerful tools for converting home equity into lifetime income because it allows you to acquire assets that keep paying long after the debt is gone.

The difference between ordinary investing and HELOC-powered investing is speed. Most people try to save money over decades before they can buy income-producing assets. A HELOC allows you to use equity that already exists to buy income now instead of later. When that income pays down the HELOC, you end up with both the asset and no debt. That is how you convert equity into income without sacrificing long-term safety.

Passive income should always be diversified. You never want your entire income to depend on one tenant, one business, or one borrower. By spreading HELOC funds across multiple cash-flowing assets, you create stability. Rental income, private lending, royalties, and digital business profits do not all behave the same way. When combined, they form a resilient income system.

Another critical concept is reinvestment. When your passive income exceeds your living expenses, you can reinvest the surplus to buy even more income. This creates compounding growth. The HELOC is simply the first fuel source. Over time, your assets become the fuel.

Eventually, something remarkable happens. Your passive income becomes so strong that you no longer need to use the HELOC at all. You may keep it available for opportunities, but your lifestyle is funded by assets. Your home has effectively financed your freedom.

This is what it means to turn real estate into a wealth engine. You are no longer waiting for appreciation. You are building income that lasts.

Practical Example: *Turning a HELOC Into Lifetime Passive Income*

Consider Linda, who owns a $600,000 home with a $320,000 mortgage. She has $280,000 in equity. At 80 percent loan-to-value, her maximum loan is $480,000. Subtracting her mortgage, she qualifies for a $160,000 HELOC. She decides to use $120,000 to build passive income while keeping $40,000 unused for safety.

Her HELOC interest rate is 8 percent. Eight percent of $120,000 is $9,600 per year, or $800 per month. Linda invests the $120,000 into three income-producing assets. She uses $60,000 for rental property down payments that generate $900 per month in net income. She uses $40,000 for private lending that pays her 10 percent annually, which equals $4,000 per year or about $333 per month. She uses the remaining $20,000 to purchase a small online business that produces $300 per month.

Linda's total monthly income is $900 plus $333 plus $300, which equals $1,533. Her HELOC costs $800 per month. After paying the HELOC interest, she has $733 left. She applies that $733 directly to the HELOC principal. After one year, she has reduced the HELOC by $8,796 because $733 times twelve equals $8,796.

Over five years, Linda's investments completely pay off the $120,000 HELOC draw. Yet her rental properties, lending notes, and business still produce $1,533 per month, which is $18,396 per year. That income is now hers for life as long as she owns the assets.

Linda has effectively turned her home equity into a permanent income stream. This is the true power of HELOC investing.

Chapter 7

Accelerating Wealth Through Strategic Reinvestment

The true power of using a HELOC to build wealth does not come from one round of investing, but from what happens after the first investments start producing income. Strategic reinvestment is the process of taking the cash flow from your assets and using it to create even more income. This is how modest equity becomes massive wealth over time. Without reinvestment, income remains linear. With reinvestment, it becomes exponential.

Most people make the mistake of treating investment income as spending money. They increase their lifestyle as soon as cash flow appears. This feels good in the short term but destroys the long-term potential of the system. When you instead reinvest that cash flow, you are effectively buying future freedom. Every dollar that goes back into your HELOC or into new assets increases the speed at which your financial engine grows.

The most efficient form of reinvestment is paying down the HELOC. When cash flow reduces the HELOC balance, your available credit increases. That new available credit can then be used to buy more income-producing assets. This is not about increasing debt. It is about increasing capacity. You are recycling the same capital over and over to create more assets.

Another powerful form of reinvestment is direct asset acquisition. Once your HELOC is partially paid down, you can use both HELOC funds and cash flow to purchase additional income streams. This creates stacking. One income stream becomes two, then three, then ten. Over time, these layers create stability and growth.

The beauty of this strategy is that it compounds quietly. No dramatic moves are required. You are simply letting money do what money does best when it is disciplined and directed. Strategic reinvestment transforms a HELOC from a funding tool into a lifelong wealth accelerator.

Practical Example: *How Reinvestment Multiplies Wealth*

Let's look at Michael, who owns a $500,000 home with a $280,000 mortgage. He has $220,000 in equity. At 80 percent loan-to-value, his maximum loan is $400,000. Subtracting his mortgage, he qualifies for a $120,000 HELOC. He uses $90,000 to start investing.

His HELOC interest rate is 8 percent, which means his annual interest is $7,200 or $600 per month. Michael invests the

$90,000 into three assets. He puts $50,000 into a rental property that produces $700 per month. He invests $25,000 into private lending that produces $300 per month. He puts $15,000 into a small digital business that produces $200 per month. His total monthly income is $1,200.

Michael uses $600 to cover the HELOC interest. That leaves $600. Instead of spending it, he reinvests it by paying down the HELOC. Over one year, he pays $7,200 toward the principal because $600 times twelve equals $7,200. His HELOC balance drops from $90,000 to $82,800.

After two years, he has paid down $14,400. Now he draws another $20,000 from the HELOC and buys another rental that produces $300 per month. His total income increases to $1,500 per month. His HELOC balance rises slightly, but his income is stronger. He continues reinvesting.

After several cycles, Michael owns multiple cash-flowing assets funded by the same home equity. His HELOC fluctuates, but his income keeps growing. Eventually, the assets pay off the HELOC and the income remains. That is the math of reinvestment.

Chapter 8

Building a Long-Term Wealth Flywheel With a HELOC

The ultimate objective of using a HELOC to build wealth is not just to create a few investments, but to build a financial flywheel that keeps generating momentum year after year. A flywheel is a system where each rotation makes the next rotation easier and faster. In financial terms, this means that every investment makes it easier to acquire the next one. When your home equity, cash flow, and reinvestment strategy are aligned, you no longer struggle to find money for opportunities. Your system produces it.

The first component of the flywheel is equity. Your home provides the initial capital. The second component is income-producing assets. These are the investments you buy with your HELOC. The third component is cash flow. This is the money those assets generate. The fourth component is reinvestment. Cash flow is used to pay down the HELOC and create new borrowing capacity. The final component is redeployment. New borrowing capacity is used to buy more assets. When these pieces work together, your wealth begins to grow on its own. What makes this flywheel so powerful is that it reduces risk over time instead of increasing it. As your

HELOC is paid down, your available credit increases and your interest costs decrease. At the same time, your income-producing assets continue generating cash. Even if markets change or opportunities slow down, the flywheel keeps turning because it is powered by existing assets, not speculation.

Another important part of the flywheel is patience. Wealth is not created in one transaction. It is created by repeating simple, disciplined actions over many years. Drawing from a HELOC, buying cash flow, applying income to the HELOC, and reinvesting is not exciting. But it is extremely effective. This is how families quietly build financial independence without taking extreme risks.

Eventually, the flywheel reaches a point where it no longer needs the HELOC to grow. Your assets are producing enough income to fund new investments on their own. At that stage, your home is no longer the primary source of capital. It simply becomes one part of a much larger financial ecosystem. That is the true end goal of this strategy.

This chapter is about seeing the bigger picture. A HELOC is not just a loan. It is the ignition key to a self-sustaining wealth machine.

Practical Example: *How a HELOC Flywheel Builds Wealth Over Time*

Consider Stephanie, who owns a $650,000 home with a $350,000 mortgage. She has $300,000 in equity. At 80 percent loan-to-value, her maximum loan is $520,000. Subtracting her mortgage, she qualifies for a $170,000 HELOC. She decides to use $120,000 to start her flywheel and keep $50,000 unused as a safety reserve.

Her HELOC interest rate is 8 percent, which means her annual interest on $120,000 is $9,600, or $800 per month. Stephanie invests the $120,000 into three income-producing assets. She puts $60,000 into rental property down payments that generate $900 per month in net income. She invests $40,000 into private lending at 10 percent annually, which produces $4,000 per year or about $333 per month. She uses the remaining $20,000 to buy a small online business that produces $300 per month.

Stephanie's total monthly cash flow is $900 plus $333 plus $300, which equals $1,533. She uses $800 to pay the HELOC interest. That leaves $733 per month. She sends that $733 back to the HELOC principal. After one year, she has reduced the HELOC by $8,796 because $733 times twelve equals $8,796. Her HELOC balance drops from $120,000 to $111,204. Because her HELOC balance is lower, she now has more available credit. She uses $20,000 of that new capacity to buy another small cash-flowing asset that produces $250 per month. Her total income increases to $1,783 per month. Her interest cost rises slightly, but her net cash flow also rises. She continues sending the excess to the HELOC.

Over several years, this cycle repeats. Her assets keep growing, her HELOC keeps getting paid down, and her income keeps increasing. Eventually, the HELOC is paid off entirely, but Stephanie owns a portfolio of assets producing several thousand dollars per month. Her home was the ignition. The flywheel now runs on its own.

Chapter 9

Knowing When to Pause, Pay Down, and Lock in Gains

Building wealth with a HELOC is not about staying in constant expansion mode. It is about knowing when to accelerate and when to stabilize. One of the most important skills in long-term wealth building is understanding when to stop drawing from your HELOC and focus on paying it down. This is what converts temporary leverage into permanent wealth. Without this phase, people remain trapped in perpetual borrowing. With it, they lock in financial security.

Every HELOC strategy moves through cycles. First you borrow and invest. Then your investments produce cash flow. Then you decide whether to deploy more capital or to reduce risk. This decision should be based on your cash-flow coverage ratio, which is how much income your investments produce compared to how much your HELOC costs. When coverage is high, you can expand. When coverage is thin, you should pause and strengthen the foundation.

The purpose of paying down the HELOC is not to eliminate opportunity. It is to eliminate fragility. The lower your HELOC balance, the lower your monthly interest and the more resilient your system becomes. When the line is mostly paid down but your assets are still producing income, your home is effectively free from risk while your wealth continues to grow.

Another reason to pause is market conditions. When investments are overpriced or unstable, it is often wiser to reduce leverage and wait. Cash flow can continue paying down the HELOC while you prepare for the next opportunity. This discipline prevents you from being forced into bad deals just because money is available.

The final stage of this process is locking in gains. This happens when the HELOC has been paid off or reduced to a level where your investments could easily cover it even in a downturn. At that point, the income becomes yours to enjoy, reinvest, or use for lifestyle. You are no longer building under pressure. You are building from a position of strength.

This chapter is about maturity in wealth building. The smartest investors know when to push and when to consolidate. That balance is what creates long-term financial freedom.

Practical Example: *How Pausing and Paying Down Creates Real Wealth*

Let's look at Brian, who owns a $580,000 home with a $320,000 mortgage. He has $260,000 in equity. At 80 percent loan-to-value, his maximum loan is $464,000. Subtracting his mortgage, he qualifies for a $144,000 HELOC. He initially uses $100,000 to build income.

His HELOC interest rate is 8 percent, so his annual interest is $8,000, or $667 per month. Brian invests the $100,000 into three income-producing assets. He uses $55,000 for rental property down payments that produce $800 per month. He invests $30,000 into private lending that produces $350 per month. He invests $15,000 into a small digital business that produces $200 per month. His total income is $1,350 per month.

After paying the $667 HELOC interest, Brian has $683 per month left. He applies this to the HELOC principal. Over one year, that equals $8,196 because $683 times twelve is $8,196. After three years, he has paid down about $24,588. His HELOC balance drops from $100,000 to about $75,412.

At this point, Brian's investments are still producing $1,350 per month, but his interest cost is now much lower because the balance is lower. His coverage ratio has improved significantly. Instead of borrowing more, he decides to pause and focus on paying down the HELOC. He sends all excess cash flow to principal.

After another three years, his HELOC is fully paid off. Brian now owns all three income-producing assets free and clear. They continue producing $1,350 per month, or $16,200 per year. His home is no longer leveraged by the HELOC, but his wealth remains.

Brian has successfully turned temporary leverage into permanent income. That is the payoff phase of HELOC investing.

Chapter 10

Turning Home Equity Into a Legacy of Wealth

Using a HELOC to build wealth is not just about increasing income during your lifetime. It is about creating a financial legacy that continues to support your family for generations. When home equity is converted into income-producing assets, those assets can be passed down, managed, and expanded long after the original HELOC is gone. This is how ordinary homes become extraordinary wealth engines.

The most powerful legacy strategy is replacing debt with assets. A HELOC is temporary. Assets are permanent. When you use your HELOC to acquire cash-flowing investments and then allow those investments to pay off the line, you end up with property, businesses, and income streams that belong to you free and clear. Those assets can be inherited, sold, or reinvested by your heirs.

Another key part of legacy planning is structure. Assets should be held in ways that make them easy to transfer. Trusts, LLCs, and proper estate planning ensure that what you build is not lost to taxes or confusion. Your HELOC strategy should be aligned with your long-term estate plan. The goal is simple.

Use leverage while you are alive to build income. Eliminate the leverage before it becomes a burden. Pass on the income, not the debt. This creates security for your family and opportunity for future generations.

This is how your home becomes more than shelter. It becomes a cornerstone of generational wealth.

Practical Example: *Creating a HELOC-Funded Legacy*

Let's look at Patricia, who owns a $700,000 home with a $350,000 mortgage. She has $350,000 in equity. At 80 percent loan-to-value, her maximum loan is $560,000. Subtracting her mortgage, she qualifies for a $210,000 HELOC. She decides to use $150,000 to build long-term income.

Her HELOC interest rate is 8 percent. Eight percent of $150,000 is $12,000 per year, or $1,000 per month. Patricia invests the $150,000 into three assets. She uses $80,000 to buy rental properties that generate $1,200 per month. She invests $50,000 into private lending at 10 percent, which produces $5,000 per year or $417 per month. She uses $20,000 to buy a small online business that produces $300 per month. Her total income is $1,917 per month.

After paying the $1,000 HELOC interest, she has $917 left. She applies that to the HELOC principal. Over one year, that equals $11,004. Over several years, her investments pay off the HELOC. Yet the assets remain.

At the end of the cycle, Patricia owns income-producing properties, lending notes, and businesses that generate nearly $2,000 per month. Her home is no longer leveraged by the HELOC, but her family now owns permanent income streams. That is how equity becomes legacy.

Chapter 11

Exiting the HELOC While Keeping the Wealth

The final phase of a successful HELOC wealth strategy is the exit. An exit does not mean walking away from opportunity. It means eliminating leverage while preserving everything that leverage helped you build. This is the moment when temporary debt is replaced by permanent income. Without a proper exit plan, even a successful investment strategy can leave unnecessary risk on the table. With an exit plan, your home becomes completely protected while your wealth remains.

Exiting a HELOC begins with understanding your true financial position. You must know how much cash flow your investments produce, how much your HELOC costs, and how quickly the balance is being reduced. When investment income consistently exceeds HELOC payments by a wide margin, you are in a strong position to accelerate the payoff of the line. This is when you shift from growth mode to consolidation mode.

Consolidation means using excess cash flow to aggressively reduce the HELOC balance. Instead of reinvesting every dollar, you direct more of it toward principal. This lowers interest costs, increases safety, and shortens the time until you are debt-free. The investments remain. Only the leverage disappears.

Another exit strategy is selective liquidation. If one investment has appreciated significantly, you may sell it and use the proceeds to pay off a large portion of the HELOC. The remaining assets then continue producing income with far less risk. This is not failure. This is harvesting.

Once the HELOC is paid off, you are in the strongest financial position possible. You own assets that generate income, and your home is no longer collateral for any of it. At that point, you can decide whether to open a new HELOC for future opportunities or simply enjoy the income your system produces.

This chapter is about completing the journey. The HELOC was the tool. The wealth is the result. The exit is what makes it permanent.

Practical Example: *Exiting a HELOC While Keeping the Income*

Let's look at Daniel, who owns a $620,000 home with a $320,000 mortgage. He has $300,000 in equity. At 80 percent loan-to-value, his maximum loan is $496,000. Subtracting his mortgage, he qualifies for a $176,000 HELOC.

He uses $120,000 to build income. His HELOC interest rate is 8 percent, which means $9,600 per year or $800 per month. Daniel invests the $120,000 into three assets. He uses $60,000 to buy rental properties that produce $900 per month. He invests $40,000 into private lending that produces $333 per month. He uses $20,000 to buy a small online business that produces $300 per month. His total income is $1,533 per month.

After paying $800 in HELOC interest, Daniel has $733 left. He sends this to the HELOC principal. Over one year, he pays $8,796. After five years, he has paid off most of the $120,000.

At this point, Daniel decides to sell one rental property for a profit of $40,000. He uses that to wipe out the remaining HELOC balance. Now the HELOC is gone, but Daniel still owns income-producing assets generating over $1,200 per month.

Daniel has successfully exited the HELOC while keeping the wealth. That is how leverage becomes freedom.

Chapter 12

Living on HELOC-Built Wealth Without Going Back to Work

The final outcome of using a HELOC to build wealth is not just owning assets, but being able to live off the income they produce. At this stage, the work has already been done. Your home equity has been converted into businesses, properties, and cash-flowing systems that pay you month after month. You are no longer relying on a paycheck. You are relying on the economic activity of assets you own. This chapter explains how to structure your financial life once you reach that stage.

The first priority is stability of income. You must ensure that your income streams are diversified and reliable. Rental income, lending income, business income, and digital royalties all behave differently. When one dips, the others often remain steady. This keeps your lifestyle protected even during economic shifts.

The second priority is preserving principal. You do not want to sell or consume the assets that generate your income. You want to live on the cash flow. This is how wealth lasts. If you spend the principal, the income disappears. If you spend the income, the principal remains. The third priority is inflation protection. Income-producing assets naturally adjust with inflation. Rents rise. Interest rates increase. Businesses raise prices. This protects your purchasing power better than savings ever could.

The final priority is flexibility. Because your home is no longer leveraged by a HELOC, you can choose to re-enter leverage if an opportunity arises or remain fully debt-free. You are in control.

This is the endgame of the HELOC wealth strategy. Your home gave you the starting capital. Your discipline built the system. Your assets now fund your life.

Practical Example: *Living on HELOC-Built Income*

Let's look at Teresa, who owns a $750,000 home with a $350,000 mortgage. She has $400,000 in equity. At 80 percent loan-to-value, her maximum loan is $600,000. Subtracting her mortgage, she qualifies for a $250,000 HELOC. Over several years, she uses $180,000 of that to build income.

Her HELOC interest rate was 8 percent, meaning $14,400 per year or $1,200 per month. Teresa invested the $180,000 into rental properties, private lending, and digital businesses that produced $2,400 per month.

She used $1,200 to pay the HELOC and the remaining $1,200 to pay down the principal. Over time, the HELOC was fully paid off. But her assets still produce $2,400 per month, or $28,800 per year.

Teresa now lives on that income. Her home is fully protected. Her wealth works for her. That is the full cycle of HELOC wealth creation.

Chapter 13

Rebuilding, Repeating, and Expanding the Wealth Cycle

The most powerful aspect of using a HELOC to build wealth is that the process never has to stop. Once you have successfully converted home equity into income and paid off the line, you are in a position that very few people ever reach. You own assets, you control cash flow, and your home is protected. From here, you can choose to repeat the cycle, expand it, or simply enjoy the income. This chapter explains how to do all three safely and intelligently.

Repeating the cycle means reopening or reusing your HELOC after it has been paid down. Because your home has likely appreciated and your mortgage has decreased, you often have even more equity available than you did the first time. This means you can run the same strategy again but at a higher level. The difference now is that you are no longer starting from zero. You already have income-producing assets from the first cycle. That income adds stability and allows you to be more selective with new investments.

Expanding the cycle means layering new sources of capital on top of your HELOC strategy. This could include business credit, partner capital, or even profits from your existing investments. When you combine these with home equity, you dramatically increase your capacity to acquire assets. The key is that every new dollar of capital must still follow the same rules: it must produce income, it must cover its own cost, and it must be manageable under stress.

Rebuilding refers to what happens when life changes. Markets shift. Families grow. Goals evolve. You may sell assets, pay down debt, or restructure your portfolio. The HELOC strategy is flexible enough to adapt. Because you control the capital and the assets, you are never locked into one rigid plan. You can always step back, consolidate, and then move forward again when conditions improve.

The reason this system works so well is that it is self-reinforcing. Assets create income. Income creates credit. Credit creates more assets. Over time, this cycle builds financial momentum that becomes harder and harder to stop. Even if you pause for years, the assets continue producing.

This chapter is about seeing the HELOC strategy not as a one-time event, but as a lifelong wealth framework. You are no longer dependent on one house, one job, or one investment. You are operating a system that can grow, contract, and grow again as your life and the economy change.

Practical Example: *Repeating and Expanding the HELOC Wealth Cycle*

Let's look at Victor, who owns a $700,000 home with a $350,000 mortgage. He has $350,000 in equity. At 80 percent loan-to-value, his maximum loan is $560,000. Subtracting his mortgage, he qualifies for a $210,000 HELOC. In his first cycle, he uses $150,000 to build income.

His HELOC interest rate is 8 percent, which equals $12,000 per year or $1,000 per month. Victor invests the $150,000 into rental properties, private lending, and digital businesses that produce $2,000 per month. After paying the $1,000 HELOC interest, he applies the remaining $1,000 to the HELOC principal. Over one year, he pays down $12,000. Over ten years, the HELOC is fully paid off.

At this point, Victor still owns assets producing $2,000 per month, or $24,000 per year. His home has also appreciated to $800,000, and his mortgage has dropped to $300,000. Now his 80 percent loan-to-value is $640,000. Subtracting his $300,000 mortgage, he qualifies for a new $340,000 HELOC.

Because Victor already has $24,000 per year in income from his first cycle, he can safely deploy more capital. He uses $200,000 of the new HELOC to acquire more income-producing assets that generate another $2,500 per month. Now his total income is $4,500 per month. His HELOC interest is about $1,333 per month. After paying that, he still has over $3,000 left.

Victor has successfully repeated and expanded the cycle. One home, used wisely over time, has created a growing financial engine that can support him for life.

Chapter 14

Creating Financial Freedom With a HELOC Lifestyle

The ultimate reward of using a HELOC to build wealth is not just financial security, but financial freedom. Financial freedom means your time is no longer controlled by a paycheck. It means you decide when to work, what to work on, and how to live. When home equity has been converted into income-producing assets and those assets have replaced the HELOC, your life begins to change in ways that go far beyond money. This chapter explains how to design a lifestyle around HELOC-built wealth so that your assets support your goals, not the other way around.

The first step in creating a HELOC lifestyle is understanding your true cost of living. Many people never calculate what it actually takes to run their household. Mortgage, taxes, insurance, food, utilities, transportation, and personal expenses all add up. When you know this number, you know how much passive income you need. The HELOC strategy allows you to target that number directly by acquiring income-producing assets until your lifestyle is fully covered. The second step is aligning income streams with your values. Some people prefer hands-on investments like rental properties. Others prefer more passive options like private lending or digital assets. A well-designed HELOC portfolio can include both. The goal is not to maximize profit at the expense of your time or peace of mind. The goal is to build income that supports the life you want to live.

The third step is gradual transition. You do not have to quit your job the moment your investments begin producing income. You can slowly reduce your reliance on earned income while increasing your reliance on passive income. This reduces stress and gives you time to adjust to a new way of living.

The fourth step is resilience. Your lifestyle should be supported by multiple income streams, not one. This ensures that a vacancy, a market change, or a business slowdown does not threaten your freedom. When your HELOC-built assets are diversified, your lifestyle becomes stable and sustainable.

The final step is optionality. Because your home is no longer burdened by a HELOC, you are free to take new opportunities or enjoy your existing income. You can reinvest, travel, spend time with family, or build new projects. Your wealth is no longer fragile. It is flexible.

This is the true purpose of using a HELOC to build wealth. It is not about accumulating numbers on a spreadsheet. It is about creating a life where money works for you instead of you working for money.

Practical Example: *Designing a HELOC-Funded Life*

Let's look at Amanda, who owns a $680,000 home with a $340,000 mortgage. She has $340,000 in equity. At 80 percent loan-to-value, her maximum loan is $544,000. Subtracting her mortgage, she qualifies for a $204,000 HELOC. Over several years, she uses $150,000 of it to build income.

Her HELOC interest rate was 8 percent, so her interest cost was $12,000 per year or $1,000 per month. Amanda invested the $150,000 into rental properties, private lending, and digital businesses that produced $2,800 per month in total.

She used $1,000 per month to pay the HELOC and $1,800 per month to pay down the principal. Over several years, the HELOC was fully paid off. Her investments still produce $2,800 per month.

Amanda's household expenses are $2,400 per month. That means her HELOC-built income now covers her entire lifestyle with $400 left over. She no longer needs a job to survive. Her home funded her freedom, and her assets now pay her to live.

Chapter 15

Making Your HELOC Wealth System Bulletproof

The difference between people who temporarily grow wealthy and those who remain wealthy for life is not how much money they make, but how well their financial systems can survive stress. A HELOC-based wealth strategy must be built to withstand economic downturns, interest rate changes, vacancies, and personal life events. This chapter explains how to make your HELOC wealth system strong enough to survive anything while continuing to grow.

The first layer of protection is excess cash flow. Your investments should always produce significantly more income than the HELOC costs. This margin allows you to absorb shocks. If interest rates rise or income temporarily falls, you still have room to operate. Thin margins are dangerous. Wide margins are safe.

The second layer of protection is reserves. You should always keep part of your HELOC unused or keep cash aside. This reserve allows you to make payments during disruptions without selling assets or panicking. Liquidity is what keeps long-term strategies alive. The third layer of protection is asset quality. Strong assets survive downturns. Housing, essential services, and income-based businesses continue to perform even when the economy slows. Speculative assets disappear when conditions tighten. When your home is backing your investments, quality is non-negotiable.

The fourth layer is diversification. Your income should come from multiple sources. One rental, one business, or one borrower should never carry the entire load. Diversification is how you prevent single points of failure.

The fifth layer is debt reduction. Even while investing, you must be paying down the HELOC over time. This continuously reduces risk. The goal is not permanent leverage. The goal is temporary leverage that creates permanent income.

When all of these layers are combined, your HELOC system becomes extremely resilient. Even in the worst-case scenario, your home is protected, your income continues, and your wealth grows.

Practical Example: *Building a Bulletproof HELOC System*

Let's look at Carlos, who owns a $720,000 home with a $360,000 mortgage. He has $360,000 in equity. At 80 percent loan-to-value, his maximum loan is $576,000. Subtracting his mortgage, he qualifies for a $216,000 HELOC.

He decides to use only $150,000 and keep $66,000 unused as reserves.

His HELOC interest rate is 8 percent, which means $12,000 per year or $1,000 per month. Carlos invests the $150,000 into three income-producing assets. He uses $80,000 for rental properties that generate $1,300 per month. He invests $40,000 into private lending that generates $400 per month. He invests $30,000 into a small business that produces $350 per month. His total monthly income is $2,050.

Carlos pays $1,000 in HELOC interest and uses the remaining $1,050 to reduce the HELOC principal. After one year, he has paid $12,600 toward the balance. His HELOC is dropping quickly while his assets keep producing income.

Even if one income stream temporarily drops, Carlos still has reserves and margin. His home is protected. His system is bulletproof.

Final Thoughts

Using a HELOC to Build Wealth

The journey you have taken through this book is not just about learning how to borrow against your home. It is about learning how to think like someone who controls capital instead of someone who is controlled by it. Most people go their entire lives never realizing that their largest financial asset, their home, could be transformed into a powerful engine for building income, businesses, and long-term security. They are taught to pay their mortgage, wait for appreciation, and hope that someday it will be enough. You now know that your home can do far more than that when used with strategy, discipline, and intention.

The true shift happens when you stop seeing debt as something to fear and start seeing it as something to manage. A HELOC, when used recklessly, can be dangerous. But when used deliberately to acquire cash-flowing assets, it becomes one of the safest and most flexible tools available to everyday homeowners. You are no longer borrowing to consume. You are borrowing to create. That one change in mindset is what separates financial stress from financial growth. Throughout this book you learned how to turn equity into working capital, how to deploy it into income-producing assets, how to recycle it through cash flow, and how to eventually exit the debt while keeping the wealth. That cycle is the heart of everything you will ever do with a HELOC. It does not matter whether you invest in rental properties, lending, digital businesses, or other cash-flowing assets. The principles remain the same. Income pays debt. Debt unlocks opportunity. Opportunity creates more income. Over time, that loop builds a system that grows even when you are not actively working.

One of the most powerful ideas you have been exposed to is that wealth is not built by how much you earn, but by how well you deploy what you control. Two people can earn the same income and end up in completely different financial positions based on what they do with their capital. A HELOC gives you access to capital that most people never realize they have. What you do with it determines everything that follows.

As a homeowner, you already have an advantage. You are not starting from zero. You have equity. You have leverage. You have a built-in financial foundation. When that foundation is paired with smart investing, risk management, and disciplined reinvestment, it becomes something extraordinary. It becomes a machine that produces money, freedom, and opportunity for decades. You do not have to become a full-time investor to use this strategy. You simply need to be intentional. You need to ensure that every dollar borrowed is tied to an asset that produces more than it costs. You need to keep reserves, diversify income, and always have an exit plan. When those rules are followed, your home stops being a liability and becomes a silent partner in your financial life.

The greatest danger is not using a HELOC. The greatest danger is leaving equity idle while inflation erodes its value and time passes. When you understand how to use home equity responsibly, you gain control over one of the most powerful wealth tools available to everyday people. That is the real gift of this book.

You now have the knowledge to turn your home into more than a place to live. You have the knowledge to turn it into a foundation for lasting wealth, stability, and freedom for you and your family. What you do next will determine how far that foundation can carry you.

How to Get a Personalized HELOC Review

If you found *HELOC Fundamentals: How Home Equity Lines of Credit Really Work — and How to Use Them Safely* helpful, you may want to see how these concepts apply to your own home, credit profile, and financial goals.

Every homeowner's situation is unique. Home value, mortgage balance, credit history, income type, and state-specific lending rules all affect how much equity you can access, what type of HELOC you may qualify for, and what terms may be available. The examples in this book are designed to teach how HELOCs work — but your real options can only be determined by reviewing your actual numbers.

If you would like a **no-obligation Home Equity Line of Credit review**, you can request one here:

Website:https://www.nodocsheloc.com

Email:info@FinibiMortgage.com

A licensed mortgage broker will review your information and explain what HELOC and home equity options may be available to you based on your specific situation.

No cost. No pressure. No obligation.

Joseph G. Correa

About the Author

Joseph G. Correa is a licensed mortgage broker and the founder of Finibi Mortgage, a Florida-based brokerage specializing in home equity, real estate investment financing, and alternative lending strategies for homeowners, business owners, and investors. With more than two decades of experience in mortgage lending, underwriting, and financial structuring, Joseph has helped thousands of borrowers access capital using intelligent, low-risk leverage rather than high-interest consumer debt.

Unlike traditional loan officers who focus only on closing transactions, Joseph's approach is rooted in long-term financial strategy. He believes that mortgages, HELOCs, and credit lines should be used as tools for building wealth, protecting cash flow, and creating financial resilience — not as traps that keep families locked into decades of unnecessary interest payments. This philosophy has made him a trusted advisor for entrepreneurs, real estate investors, and self-employed borrowers who need flexible, modern financing solutions that banks often fail to provide.

Joseph is widely known for his expertise in home equity lines of credit, no-documentation and bank-statement loan programs, investor financing, and creative equity-based strategies such as debt-elimination systems and capital recycling. His ability to translate complex lending rules into simple, actionable guidance has helped homeowners turn idle equity into productive capital for investments, businesses, and passive income.

Through his education platform, Finibi Academy, Joseph has trained tens of thousands of students worldwide in credit, mortgage strategy, real estate financing, and financial independence. His courses and books are used by first-time homeowners, seasoned investors, and financial professionals seeking a clearer, more honest understanding of how modern lending really works.

Joseph created *The Home Equity Wealth Series* to give everyday homeowners the same financial knowledge that banks, hedge funds, and institutional investors use to control capital and minimize risk. His mission is simple: to help people stop guessing, stop fearing debt, and start using smart leverage to build real financial freedom.

When he is not structuring loans or writing, Joseph works with families and investors across the United States to design personalized equity strategies that align with their goals, cash flow, and long-term wealth plans.

The Home Equity Wealth Series Roadmap

The Professional Guide to Using Your Home to Build Financial Freedom

The purpose of *The Home Equity Wealth Series* is to give homeowners the same financial tools and strategies used by banks, investors, and institutions—translated into clear, practical guidance for everyday people. Each book builds on the last, taking you from basic understanding to advanced mastery of how to use home equity safely, intelligently, and profitably across every stage of life.

Book 1 — *HELOC Fundamentals*This book gives you the foundation. You will understand how Home Equity Lines of Credit work, how they are structured, how risk is controlled, and how equity becomes usable capital. The books that follow are designed to help you apply that knowledge to your own situation, your income type, your credit profile, and your long-term financial goals.

Book 2 — *How to Qualify for a HELOC* This book shows you how lenders actually evaluate borrowers. You will learn how credit scores, income, property type, and debt ratios affect approval, limits, and interest rates. You will also learn how to position yourself to qualify for the largest possible credit line at the best possible terms.

Book 3 — *HELOCs for Real Estate Investors* This book focuses on using home equity to buy, rehab, refinance, and scale rental properties. It explains how investors use HELOCs for down payments, renovations, and portfolio growth while keeping cash flow positive and risk controlled.

Book 4 — *Self-Employed HELOC Strategies* Designed for business owners, freelancers, 1099 borrowers, and LLCs, this book explains how bank-statement income, business income, and alternative documentation can be used to qualify for home equity even when traditional tax returns do not reflect true cash flow.

Book 5 — *Credit Mastery for HELOC Approval* This book dives deep into credit strategy. You will learn how utilization, credit mix, and reporting behavior affect HELOC limits and pricing—and how to optimize your credit profile specifically for home equity approval.

Book 6 — *No-Doc & Alternative HELOC Programs* This book covers asset-based HELOCs, no-income-verification options, and non-traditional lending programs for high-net-worth, self-employed, or cash-heavy borrowers who do not fit inside standard underwriting models.

Book 7 — *Using a HELOC to Eliminate Debt* This book teaches how to use home equity to replace high-interest credit cards, personal loans, and auto loans with low-interest revolving credit, allowing borrowers to eliminate debt years faster and save tens of thousands of dollars in interest.

Book 8 — *Using a HELOC to Build Wealth* This book shows how homeowners fund investments, businesses, and passive income streams using HELOCs while maintaining liquidity and controlling risk.

Book 9 — *HELOC Risk Management* This book focuses entirely on safety. You will learn how to structure buffers, cash-flow coverage, rate protection, and leverage limits so your home becomes safer over time—not more vulnerable.

Book 10 — *The Smart Borrower's Home Equity Blueprint* The final book ties everything together into a complete lifetime strategy for using home equity as a personal banking system, investment engine, and financial safety net.

Book 11 — *The Cashflow Accelerator Method*

The Cashflow Accelerator Method is the final transformation stage of *The Home Equity Wealth Series*. While the earlier books teach how to access, qualify for, and safely use home equity, this book teaches how to **weaponize cash flow itself** to permanently eliminate debt and create lasting wealth. Together, these books are designed to turn a single asset—your home—into a lifelong financial advantage. Each volume adds another layer of understanding, allowing you to move from homeowner to capital manager, from borrower to strategist, and from financial stress to long-term stability.

This is not about taking more risk.It is about learning how money really works—and using that knowledge to build financial freedom that lasts.

Educational & Financial Disclaimer

This book is provided for **educational and informational purposes only**. The author and publisher are not engaged in rendering legal, tax, accounting, investment, or financial advice. Although the author is a licensed mortgage broker, the information in this book is intended to provide general education about Home Equity Lines of Credit (HELOCs) and home equity strategy, not personalized financial, legal, or lending advice.

Mortgage programs, underwriting guidelines, interest rates, credit requirements, and home equity products vary by lender, investor, state, and economic conditions, and may change at any time without notice. The examples, calculations, and scenarios presented in this book are hypothetical and are for illustration only. They do not represent guaranteed outcomes or actual loan approvals.

Before making any financial decisions, including applying for a HELOC, refinancing, borrowing against home equity, or using credit for investment or debt repayment, readers should consult with a qualified mortgage professional, financial advisor, tax advisor, or attorney who can evaluate their specific situation.

Risk Disclosure

Borrowing against home equity involves risk. A HELOC is secured by your home, which means failure to make required payments could result in foreclosure or loss of property. This book teaches responsible, conservative, and structured use of home equity, but no financial strategy is risk-free.

Readers are solely responsible for their financial decisions. Neither the author nor the publisher makes any warranties, express or implied, about the accuracy, completeness, or applicability of the information in this book to any individual or situation.

www.ingramcontent.com/pod-product-compliance
Ingram Content Group UK Ltd.
Pitfield, Milton Keynes, MK11 3LW, UK
UKHW020156290926
15471UKWH00005B/905

9 798295 576553